Preparing for the LCCI Exam

WRITTEN ENGLISH FOR BUSINESS

Second level

R G H Andrews

OXFORD UNIVERSITY PRESS

Oxford University Press
Walton Street, Oxford OX2 6DP

Oxford   New York   Toronto   Madrid   Delhi
Bombay   Calcutta   Madras   Karachi   Kuala Lumpur
Singapore Hong Kong   Tokyo   Nairobi   Dar es Salaam
Cape Town Melbourne   Auckland

and associated companies in
Berlin   Ibadan

OXFORD and OXFORD ENGLISH are trade marks of
Oxford University Press

ISBN 0 19 451233 9
© Oxford University Press 1990
First published 1990
Third impression 1993

Set by Oxford University Press
Printed in Hong Kong

All rights reserved. No part of this publication may be reproduced, stored in a retrieval system, or transmitted, in any form or by any means, electronic or otherwise, without the prior permission of Oxford University Press.

This book is sold subject to the condition that it shall not, by way of trade or otherwise, be lent, re-sold, hired out, or otherwise circulated without the publisher's prior consent in any form of binding or cover other than that in which it is published and without a similar condition including this condition being imposed on the subsequent purchaser.

CONTENTS

                                                  Page

Introduction 5
  1 How to use this book 5
  2 What the examiner is looking for 6
  3 Sample paper 7

Question 1 10
  A The Memo 10
  B The Report 16
  C The Leaflet 23
  D The Notice 28
  E The Article 32

Question 2: the Letter 37

Question 3: Reformulation 47
  A Reduction 47
  B Expansion 52

INTRODUCTION

1 HOW TO USE THIS BOOK

This book is suitable both for class use, under the guidance of a teacher, and for people studying alone.

If you are studying by yourself, read the information given very carefully and make notes of any points which you do not understand fully and of any of your own weaknesses which are mentioned. Read these notes frequently until you do understand these points and have overcome your weaknesses.

The next section in this Introduction tells you what the examiner is looking for when marking your script. You should study this with great care. Many candidates lose marks in this examination by writing what they *think* the examiner wants rather than what is really wanted. You can avoid this by reading this Introduction carefully, and by taking the time in the examination to read each question to find exactly what the examiner requires.

At the end of the Introduction is a complete past examination paper. This shows you the kinds of questions that you will face in the examination. Note that in Question 1, you have a choice, and have to attempt *only one* of the tasks given.

After the Introduction, the book takes the three types of question in the paper in turn. This is how you can use the different sections for each of the three questions:

- Read the Sample Question.
- Read the 'Approach' section.
- Write your answer to the Sample Question, without using this book.
- Compare your answer with the Sample Answers and Comments to get an idea of the standard that you have reached (and remember that Model Answers are examples, not the *only* possible answers).
- Read the Summary of Common Errors.
- Answer the Further Practice questions.

For further practice, you might then attempt the complete past paper at the end of the Introduction. Other past papers can be obtained from the London Chamber of Commerce Examinations Board, to enable you to practise not only individual questions but also the effective use of time under examination conditions.

Finally, bear in mind that grammar, spelling, punctuation and paragraphing are important in every kind of question.

2 WHAT THE EXAMINER IS LOOKING FOR

What is the examiner looking for when marking an English for Business Second Level script?

- First, the examiner expects candidates to *read the instructions* on the question paper and *then carry them out*. This sounds simple, but often it is not done. For example, in the first question, the candidate is told to carry out *one* out of *three* tasks. Candidates who try to do two or three tasks will gain no extra marks on Question 1, but they will waste time that they could be spending on Questions 2 and 3. Again, if a question asks for a memorandum (usually called a 'memo'), the examiner does not expect an essay, report, or letter: yet this error frequently happens.

- Next, the candidate is expected to know the *correct layout* of business documents such as letters, memos, and reports, and to *write them legibly*.

- Third, the examiner expects answers to fulfil their purpose, that is, to *deal adequately with the task that is set*. For example, if a question requires a letter asking for a debt to be paid immediately, the letter should be laid out correctly, keep to the point without any irrelevant matter, and be of the correct tone - in this case, firm but tactful.

- Fourth, *correct English* is of the greatest importance throughout the examination. Candidates should therefore pay great attention to grammar, paragraphing, punctuation and spelling. The business world normally expects these to be perfect at all times. All the questions award high marks for correct English. One common fault which the examiner always penalizes is the misspelling of a word that is on the question paper.

One final point. You are, of course, allowed to use words from the question paper in your answer. But the examiner does not wish to see the question copied from the question paper, with one or two words altered, and offered as an 'answer'. A surprising number of candidates try this. It always fails.

Good luck!

3 SAMPLE PAPER

SECOND LEVEL

THE LONDON CHAMBER OF COMMERCE
ENGLISH FOR BUSINESS

(CODE No: 2041)

INSTRUCTIONS TO CANDIDATES

(a) Answer all **three** questions
(b) Credit will be given for correct spelling, punctuation and grammar.
(c) Adequate and appropriate communication is required rather than a particular number of words.
(d) When you finish, check your work carefully.

QUESTION 1

Write on ONE of the following subjects:

(a) Jane Simmonds, Personnel Manager of Alpha Electronics, 80-90 Zeus Street, Manchester GG73 6LP, says to you, "Will you write a **memo** from me to Simon Clark, my deputy, please? When he returns from holiday next Monday I shall be starting a three-day conference at Harrogate. Ask him to interview the four candidates for the clerical vacancy in the Mailing Section on Monday, starting 2.30 p.m. He should make an appointment if there is a suitable candidate. The candidates have been invited for interview and their application forms and references are in the middle drawer of my desk. I'll leave my desk keys with you. On Tuesday at 10 a.m. Gerry Rhodes, the union rep., has an appointment to see me. If Simon can deal with whatever he wants, I shall be grateful. If not, I'll make another appointment to see Gerry when I'm back on Thursday." *Write the correctly laid out memo.*

(b) You and your colleagues at work have complained to the management that, as the number of staff in your office has trebled over the past two years, the staff canteen gets uncomfortably overcrowded during the lunch break between 12 noon and 1 p.m. Several suggestions for overcoming the problem have been put forward by members of staff, such as enlarging the canteen, the issuing of luncheon vouchers* so that fewer people use the canteen and staggering the break instead of everybody having lunch at the same time. Write a **report** of the situation and its possible solutions, stating the one you favour, and why, to the General Manager.

(c) Your company will be moving to another site next month. Write a **leaflet** which can be distributed to customers, informing them of the date of the move, the new address, for how long – if at all – it will affect the smooth running of the business, and any other information you think is required.

*Luncheon vouchers, representing a fixed, small amount of money, are issued by employers to employees to enable them to buy meals at certain restaurants or other eating places.

(40 marks)

QUESTION 2

Your company, Alpha Electronics, has received the following letter. Write a correctly laid out letter in reply **after you have read the memo below,** which your Office Manager gives to you.

Telephone (75613) 19283

Offices Complete
Temple House
Church Avenue
Cheltenham
Gloucestershire
AX12 X55

Ref: AE/1/JL/WBS
Alpha Electronics
80-90 Zeus Street
Manchester
GG73 6LP

21 April 1989

Dear Sirs,

Alpha Electronic Typewriter Model AET 524

We have sold six of the above typewriters out of the thirty you sent to us on 10 April this year. All the purchasers have complained that after about six to seven hours' use the machines stopped working. Our mechanics were unable to find what had caused this breakdown.

This has never happened with any other models of yours.

We should be pleased to receive your advice on this matter at once so that we can explain to our customers what has happened.

Please treat this matter as urgent.

Yours faithfully,

James Lyon
Sales Manager

MEMORANDUM

From:	L Blythe Managing Director	**Date:** 21 April 1989
To:	Tom Paton Office Manager	**Subject:** Typewriter AET 524 **Ref:** ALPHA

I've just heard there's a fault in the above. On Monday draft a letter asking customers for <u>all</u> these machines to be returned at our expense. Apologise profusely. They will not be out of pocket because of this. Explain the machines will be modified and returned within ten days of our receiving them. As compensation, extra 10% discount will be given on customers' next three orders. Letter in my name.

(30 marks)

INTRODUCTION

QUESTION 3

Your employer is giving a talk entitled "Running Your Own Business" at a local club. She says to you, "Will you please *list* the main points about being your own boss and the misconceptions people have about it from this leaflet? It will help me in giving my talk." Complete the task

THE LEAFLET

There are all kinds of reasons for wanting to be your own boss. Some people like the idea of there being no one in authority over them, telling them what to do, saying their work is not up to standard, turning down their ideas, or insisting on methods that seem pointless. Others are attracted by the thought of deciding their own hours, or days, of work.

Running your own business gives you the status of being self-employed, perhaps also of being a company director. There is the general feeling of independence, and that your income - and perhaps even your way of life - is in your own hands. Some are attracted to the idea of starting a small enterprise and making it grow, much as a gardener tends his plot and makes a number of plants come to maturity, each in turn creating further growth.

If you are your own boss, say some people, work is so much more pleasant. You can get someone else to do the less interesting jobs and you are not bogged down in annoying details. Work becomes easier, too, because you can get someone else to do the more difficult tasks.

Many others want to set up a little business of their own to occupy their spare time, and as a pleasant way of earning extra money from work they like doing.

These are just a few of the reasons commonly given. Some have good sense behind them; others are based on completely false ideas. Most contain some element of truth which gets magnified out of all proportion, and seized upon without it being borne in mind that there are other points to consider as well.

As with so much else in life, running an enterprise of your own entails disadvantages as well as advantages. It is surprising how rarely people stop to consider in real detail just what the drawbacks are, yet this is an essential first step for anyone thinking about whether it is even practicable for him to be his own boss.

An important reason why there is such glamour about being in charge of your own business is that when you are working for someone else, many of the petty irritations of life, as well as the chore of often having to get down to work that you do not feel like doing at that particular time, become associated with being an employee. There is a feeling that, if only you were your own boss, life would immediately become infinitely pleasurable and free from irksome detail.

This is almost entirely misleading. Many of the little annoyances probably have nothing to do with being an employee: being interrupted when you have at last immersed yourself in some disagreeable task, missing the bus when you are in a hurry, feeling tired or in other ways not really up to working hard at the moment, and so on.

These occur just as much when you are your own master. In fact, they tend to happen much more often, while at the same time, their effects can be far more upsetting.

There are very real drawbacks to running your own business, though for the right kind of person, immeasurable benefits also.

(30 marks)

QUESTION 1

As you will have seen from the past paper, there are three tasks in Question 1, of which you have to choose *only one*. You may find any of the following tasks in Question 1:

A   The Memo
B   The Report
C   The Leaflet
D   The Notice
E   The Article.

We will look at each of these tasks in turn.

A The Memo

1 SAMPLE QUESTION

Europart Ltd., of Unit 26, Frilford Industrial Estate, Southolt SJ4 7DB, distributes parts for motor vehicles from its branches throughout Europe. You work in the Hanover branch.

Your manager, Peter Henig, says to you, 'We've got problems with our delivery dates. You know we guarantee delivery of any vehicle part to the shop here within 48 hours of a customer placing an order - or the customer gets a 20 per cent discount. That's one of our main selling points. Well, we've been having to offer a lot too many discounts on parts we have to get from Southolt - they often take 3 days, sometimes even a week to get here. It's not good enough.

'Could you find out what's going on? Write a **memo** under my name. Send it by fax to David Walsh, the Warehouse Manager at Southolt. Tell him what the problem is, and ask him what he's going to do about it. But be tactful. He's usually very good - and I know it's not easy to handle about 50,000 different parts. See if there are any problems at his end that he's sorting out - or if there's anything we can do to help. Is our ordering clear enough? Or perhaps he should change his express courier. But get him to say when we're going to get a normal service. We're not the only people distributing vehicle parts - there's plenty of competition if our customers want to look elsewhere.

'I'm off to a conference today, and I'll be away for a week. Tell David that if he wants to discuss anything, he can talk to you, or he can wait until I get back'.

Write the required memo.

QUESTION 1: THE MEMO

2 APPROACH

1. *Read the question twice at least*: the first time to get a general idea of what it is about, and the second time to study it in detail. You should then be able to answer the question, 'What *exactly* am I asked to do?' For our example, the answer is 'Write a tactful memo to a member of staff'.

2. Next you have to remember the correct *layout* of a memo. *At the top*, all memos include the following four pieces of information:

   From   *(sender's name and/or position in company)*
   To   *(addressee's name and/or position in company)*
   Date   *(the date the memo is written)*
   Subject   *(very briefly, what the memo is about)*

   In addition, you may need to include a heading for Reference. Finally, if you are sending the memo by fax, you should also indicate the number of pages. *At the bottom*, you may put the sender's initials, but never a signature.

3. Decide on the *correct tone* for the memo. It is clear in this question that Peter Henig is not satisfied with David Walsh's performance. But he asks for a *tactful* memo. He wants Walsh to sort out the problem, not to feel hurt. Even if the sender is quite angry, a tactful memo will usually produce a better result than an aggressive one.

4. A memo should include *relevant material only*. Decide from the question what you think is relevant. Leave out material that the addressee already knows (in this case, that Europart guarantee delivery within 48 hours of an order). And leave out material that has nothing to do with the subject of the memo.

5. *Make a list* - either on the question paper or in your answer book - of the points that you are going to make. Order the points logically in paragraphs. This order will not necessarily be the order in which the points appear in the question. If you use your answer book to make your list, neatly cross it out when you have finished referring to it.

6. Write your answer.

7. When you have finished, *read your memo right through*. Make sure that you have included all the essential points and omitted all inessential ones.

8. *Check your work for accurate English*. If you discover any errors, neatly cross them out and add the corrections.

3 MODEL ANSWER

> *From:* Peter Henig (Manager, Hanover) *Date: 2.11.90*
> *To:* David Walsh (Warehouse Manager, Southolt)
> *Subject:* Delayed deliveries *Number of pages: 1*
>
> I am sending this by fax because I am off to a conference today and will not be able to call you before I go.
>
> The problem is this: many of our orders from Southolt are arriving late. In fact, some take a week to get here. That means we are having to give our 20 per cent discount to a large number of customers – and some of them may soon start looking elsewhere.
>
> I know it is not a simple thing to stock so many parts, and your warehouse usually performs very well indeed. But we need to sort this out. Are there any problems at your end at present? Is your courier working normally?
>
> Or is there anything we can do to help?
>
> Do please contact **(write your own name here)** if there are any points you wish to raise this week. Otherwise, I will be happy to talk things over after my return.
>
> PH

4 COMMENTS ON MODEL ANSWER

1 LAYOUT

This answer has all the headings required in a memo, and would receive full marks for layout.

2 CONTENT AND EFFECTIVENESS

This answer would also win high marks for content, for the following reasons:

- It is tactful, as Peter Henig required. Walsh is not held personally responsible for the late arrival of the parts, and Henig praises his normal performance.
- The points are ordered logically. This is an important part of a good answer. Many candidates simply repeat points in the order in which they appear in the question. This is not always appropriate.
- The opening paragraph explains, without wasting words, why Henig is writing to Walsh and not trying to call him.
- The main point of the memo - delays in deliveries - is made clearly but tactfully in the second paragraph.
- Possible reasons for late deliveries are given in the third paragraph.
- Finally, Henig tactfully suggests a talk on his return from the conference.

QUESTION 1: THE MEMO

3 MECHANICAL ACCURACY

This answer would receive high marks for grammar, paragraphing, punctuation and spelling.

This piece of work would be of Distinction standard.

5 SECOND ANSWER

> From: Peter Henig
> To: David Walsh (Warehouse Manager)
>
> We distribute parts for motor vehicules and we have a problem. We garantee to get parts for costomers, if we don't we must pay 20 per cent to them for our selling point. Well, we are paying a lot too many discounts on parts we get from Southolt – they often take 3 days, sometimes even a week to get here. It's not good enough. See if there is any problems at his end or if we can do to help. We could change his express courier. We're not the only people distributing vehicule parts and we must keep our promise to costomers. I have to go to a conference today and will be away for a weak so that David can talk to you or wait until I get back.
> Yours faithfully
>
> Peter Henig

QUESTION 1: THE MEMO

6 COMMENTS ON SECOND ANSWER

1 LAYOUT

This is worth very few marks because the date and subject have been left out. *Yours faithfully* and *Peter Henig* are not required.

2 CONTENT AND EFFECTIVENESS

Very few marks would be given here for the following reasons:

- Much has been copied from the question: the writer has shown no originality.
- The candidate has included irrelevant material, such as the information on the firm's business. The recipient of the memo, David Walsh, works for Europarts and knows this.
- The candidate makes no attempt to write the memo in logical order.
- Copying from the question, the candidate writes *about* Walsh when he should be writing *to* him.
- The candidate misunderstands one suggested solution to the problem - it is for Walsh, not Henig, to change couriers.
- The candidate's use of conversational phrases like *Well,...* and *It's not good enough* means that the right tone is not achieved.

3 MECHANICAL ACCURACY

This would earn very few, or even no, marks because there are no paragraphs and the spelling (*moter*, *costomer* ...) is very poor indeed.

This piece of work would definitely fail.

7 SUMMARY OF COMMON ERRORS

These mistakes occur frequently in examination scripts. You should avoid them.

- Incorrect layout. Adding *Dear Sir, Yours faithfully*, or a signature.
- Missing out part(s) of the layout: all four main headings (*From*, *To*, *Date*, and *Subject*) are essential in all memos.
- Copying the exact words of the question paper directly into the memo.
- Not arranging the content of the memo in a logical order.
- Omitting essential pieces of information.
- Incorrect tone: unless you want to reprimand somebody *severely*, be friendly and courteous.
- Errors of grammar, paragraphing, punctuation and spelling.

QUESTION 1: THE MEMO

8 FURTHER PRACTICE

1. Your Office Manager says to you, 'I want you to write a **memo**, under my name, to staff. I have received complaints from the Canteen Supervisor about the state the staff leave the canteen in after lunch break. Many of them do not return their trays to the canteen staff, and cigarette ash and paper wrappings are left on the floor and tablecloths. Last Friday there was a large burn in a tablecloth - obviously caused by a cigarette - but nobody reported it. The canteen staff are grumbling about this - I sympathise with them. Tell staff they must keep their canteen clean; it doesn't take much time. I hope I do not have to remind them about this again.

   'By the way, if there are any accidents in the canteen, staff must report them to the Canteen Supervisor.'

2. Rainer Kruger, General manager of the Dresden branch of Universal Sports Equipment, for whom you work, says to you 'An emergency has arisen at our main British branch in Manchester - a problem with the unions. Bill Stevens, our manager there, would like me to go over and see him as soon as possible. Unfortunately, I have to go to an important meeting in a few minutes. So send him a **memo** under my name; send it by fax. Say I'll flyover later tonight. Ask him to arrange a meeting between ourselves and the union reps for two o'clock tomorrow afternoon. I'll arrive at Bill's office about nine tomorrow morning and he and I can discuss the problem before we meet the union reps. I'll leave Bill to decide whether or not he wants anybody else at our morning meeting apart from ourselves. Offer him my sympathy because this is the second problem he's had with the unions in a month. Poor fellow!'

   Write the required memo.

3. Next month, you are going on a tour of your firm's offices in the Far East with your boss, Francis Clerc. Your visit to Tokyo was scheduled to last from the 12th to the 16th inclusive. This morning Francis Clerc said to you 'Look, we're going to need more time for this trip. I'll want an extra three days in Singapore, and four days in Hong Kong. That means we'll arrive a week late in Tokyo. Could you fax a **memo** to Tokyo - that'll be to Yasuhiro Abe, the Office Manager there - and tell him? Ask him to send someone to meet us at Narita Airport on the same flight - JAL 3101 from Hong Kong, arriving at 6PM local time, a week later. Ask him to let us know that he can do that. Oh - and you'd better get him to change our hotel reservations and our meetings schedule too. And ask him to book us an extra two days in Fukuoka at the end of our time in Tokyo, and to fix up meetings with possible suppliers there. Oh, one more thing - if Howard Davis is back at work yet, could Yasuhiro get us an appointment with him?'

   Write the appropriate memo to send by fax to Mr Abe.

4. Write a **memo** to the senior night watchman of the company for which you work, telling him that the local police have informed you that there have been several burglaries in the area recently and that extra alertness is necessary. Ask him to tell his four assistants about this. Remind him that half-hourly patrols of the company must be done. Remind him also that tomorrow at 10 a.m. he must attend a meeting in your office to discuss methods of tightening the security system of the company. He must also remind his assistants that the burglar alarm must be checked six times during the night.

B The report

1 SAMPLE QUESTION

Ms Anne Woods, your Office Manager, asks you to write a **report** for her, as soon as possible, on the increase in lateness of many office staff over the last two months.

Write the correctly laid out report.

2 APPROACH

1 THE TASK

Read the question two or three times so that you know *exactly* what you are required to do. You have to write a report and, as you are not given any background material on which to base it, you have to *use your imagination and invent information*.

2 LAYOUT

There are many possible ways to set out a report. One simple layout useful in many cases is the following:

- Terms of reference

State what you are reporting on, who asked you to make the report, and the date by which the report is required if you are given one.

- Proceedings

What action(s) you took to collect the facts concerning the subject of the report.

- Findings

The facts you discovered. It may be helpful to number these, although you will not be penalized if you do not.

- Conclusions

What you, the writer of the report, think about the facts. Only comments which will be useful to the person who commissioned the report (Ms Anne Woods in our example) should be made. You may find it helpful, as with the Findings, to number these.

- Recommendations

Your practical suggestions as to what should be done (to help the office staff arrive at work on time in our example).

You then sign the report and put your position in the company in brackets underneath your signature. Finally add the date.

3 CONTENT

When you come to write the report, the terms of reference are in the question so this part of the report has already been done for you.

You must invent the content of the remainder of the report. In our example it would seem obvious that the action to be taken (proceedings) would be to question the staff who are late as to why this lateness has occurred over the last two months and then to check their excuses or reasons. From here your imagination should carry you through.

As in the answers to all questions, nothing irrelevant should be included.

List the points you are going to make under each heading either on the question paper or your answer book; if on the latter, cross them out neatly when you have finished working with them. Check that you have used correct English.

3 MODEL ANSWER

Report on the increase in lateness of some office staff over the last two months

Terms of reference

Miss Anne Woods, Office Manager, has asked me to write this report on the increase in lateness of some of the office workers over the last two months and to submit it to her as soon as possible.

Proceedings

I questioned all the office staff individually, asking why there was this sudden increase in unpunctuality, and then checked their replies.

Findings

1. The latecomers are those who travel to work by private transport and public road transport. Those who travel by train arrive on time.

2. The two main roads leading into town have had major road works done on them for the last eight weeks; this causes unavoidable traffic jams and long delays.

3. About two months ago our company opened its new mail order section. Approximately sixty new employees were recruited. As this new section starts work forty-five minutes before the office staff each morning, the car park gets filled with vehicles belonging to workers in that section. The company has not enlarged the car park to accommodate the additional vehicles. Consequently, many office staff cannot find parking space and have to drive around surrounding roads looking for a parking area.

4. I gathered the above information from my individual interviews with staff, and confirmed that it was true by observing the two main roads and the company's car park early every morning for a week.

Conclusions

Obviously, nothing can be done about the road works. I understand that they will be finished in six weeks' time.

As people will insist on travelling to work in their own transport, I think the solution is for the company either to enlarge the existing car park or to obtain another one near the office.

Recommendations

As the road works will be finished in six weeks, I suggest that staff be asked to leave home for work a little earlier than usual for this period to enable them to arrive on time. I recommend that the company enlarge the existing car park as it is surrounded by company land which at present is fenced off from the car park.

(write your own name here)   12 September 1990

Deputy Office Manager

QUESTION 1: THE REPORT

4 COMMENTS ON MODEL ANSWER

1 LAYOUT

All the sections are clearly shown and identified and the document is signed and dated. Full marks.

2 CONTENT AND EFFECTIVENESS

This would earn high marks under this heading for the following reasons:

- All of the content is relevant to the purpose of the report. Nothing inessential has been included.
- It achieves its purpose: it gives reasons why staff have been late, and offers a solution to the problem.
- It is easily readable.

3 MECHANICAL ACCURACY

High marks for correct English.

Note

In this report two reasons for the lateness of staff are given - road works and the recent expansion in demand for the car park. Two good, substantial reasons are enough. Including more reasons would not be necessary, and would use up valuable examination time.

5 SECOND ANSWER

<u>Report on the increase in lateness of the office staff</u>

<u>Terms of reference</u>

Report on increase in lateness of office staff

<u>Proceedings</u>

I asked staff individualy why thay had sudenly started coming late to work.

<u>Findings</u>

Their are road work on the too main roads coming in town and trafic jams are corsed. Our car park is fool as office staff come to work later than the workers. There are long deelays because of the trafic meating the road work. The comany car park has not bin made any biger to take the extra cars. I think we sould have a biger car park to take the extra cars. These too resons are causing the staff to be late for work.

<u>Recomendations</u>

Staff could leave for work earler to get here on time. Why cant the car park be biger. The company can aford to pay for it to be made biger. It sould be biger.

QUESTION 1: THE REPORT 21

6 COMMENTS ON SECOND ANSWER

1 LAYOUT

The candidate offers no conclusions, and fails to sign and date the report. This would score approximately half marks for layout.

2 CONTENT AND EFFECTIVENESS

This would score low marks for the following reasons:

- Part of the terms of reference has been left out: it should be *some* office staff, not all, as is implied here. The writer also forgot to add *over the last two months*.
- The findings are not reported in logical sequence. The writer has mixed the comments on the road works and the car park. It is not at all clear what the writer wants to say.
- The recommendations should be *practical* suggestions; these are not. Stating that the company can afford to enlarge the car park is irrelevant to the report.

3 MECHANICAL ACCURACY

Poor spelling throughout would ensure that few marks were awarded here.

A definite failure.

7 SUMMARY OF COMMON ERRORS

Many scripts suffer from the following errors - which have been mentioned previously.

- Incorrect layout. Omitting the section headings. Not signing and dating the report.
- Omitting to include the terms of reference; without these the report will gain few marks.
- Including irrelevant material. This is particularly easy to do when writing a report.
- Not reporting findings or recommendations in logical order.
- Poor grammar, paragraphing, punctuation and spelling.

8 FURTHER PRACTICE

1. James Gordon, Managing Director of World Audio-Visual Productions, Birmingham, has contacted the Paris branch of the company, where you work, asking for a **report** to be sent to him advising him whether or not it would be possible to have the Paris factory operate two shifts a day instead of the present one. He asks you to take workers' opinions into account when writing the report.

    Write the correctly laid out report.

2. James Gates, Office Manager of the company for which you work, says to you 'I have just been told that the directors of the company are willing to spend a large amount of money on staff education. This can be full- and part-time courses, both for general and vocational education. I'd like you to write a **report** for me as soon as possible stating what degree of staff co-operation and enthusiasm there is for such a scheme. I'd like the report as soon as possible, please, so that I can inform the directors whether or not the scheme will succeed.'

    Write an appropriate report.

3. Your Office Manager says to you, 'We have had fifty two per cent staff turnover during the past year and I am very concerned about it. Will you write a **report** on it for me, please?'

    Write the required report.

4. There have been four minor accidents in your office over the last three weeks and the Office Manager is worried. He asks you to write him a **report**, as soon as possible, on safety in the office, including staff suggestions for improving it.

    Write a correctly laid out report.

5. 'Our parent company in London have said we can develop the large piece of vacant land at the back of our offices,' says José Teruel, General Manager of Mowat Technology, Seville. 'I have had suggestions as to its use: some people think it should be turned into a garden with seats for staff to sit during breaks and after work; others that it would be better as a sports hall and social club for staff. I'd like to hear what the staff think about it. Would you write a **report** on the matter, please, that I can send to the London office to get their permission to spend the money that will be needed?'

    Write the appropriate report.

QUESTION I

C The leaflet

1 SAMPLE QUESTION

You work for a major department store - Babylone, at 40-60, rue René Coty, 75006 Paris. It is June, and you are planning the summer sale, due to last from 2nd to 20th July. Your manager, Georges Herbert, says to you 'We should have a **leaflet** in English about the sale to distribute to tourists - they don't usually come in here much, but a bit of publicity would help. Tell them we have English-speaking staff - well, not all of them, but most of the assistants can manage a few sentences. You know our main reductions - 40 per cent off furniture and leather goods, 25-50 per cent off men's and women's summer fashions, 20 per cent off bicycles, sports and camping equipment, kitchen equipment, perfumes, ... oh yes, and there's that special purchase of Beaujolais at 120 francs a case. We want to get rid of that quickly. Remember to put our opening hours in - 10 to 7, six days a week, except the 14th. See what you can do'.

Write the required leaflet.

2 APPROACH

1   You should *read* the leaflet question, like any other, two or three times so that you know *exactly* what to do. The purpose of this leaflet, as the question shows, is both to inform people about the Babylone sale and to persuade them to come and buy something. Your task is to give readers enough information to achieve this purpose, but not so many words that they lose interest.

2   *List* the points you intend to make, either on the question paper or on your answer book. If you use the answer book, do not forget to delete them when you have finished referring to them. The question gives you some material to include in the leaflet. You can also, if you wish, invent extra material and include that. But such extra material must be relevant.

3   Decide on the *layout* of your leaflet, and the *order* in which you want to make your points. No particular layout is required as it is in the memo or the report, so you have plenty of freedom here. The important thing is that it should catch the eye, be easy to read, and contain an address and a date. If these are not included in the question, you should invent them.

4   When you have finished writing, *check your answer thoroughly* for correct English.

3 MODEL ANSWER

> *The best of France is at Babylone ....*
> *and now it's at a price anyone can afford!*
> Treat yourself to some Parisian style at our summer sale, 2nd-20th July inclusive.
> Our friendly, English-speaking staff will help you find the bargain you want, including –
>
> 30% off top brands of perfume
>
> 40% off leather goods
>
> up to 50% off men's and women's summer fashions
>
> There are top-quality souvenirs for everyone at Babylone! For that extra item to take on holiday ....
> 20% off our sports and camping equipment, bicycles, and kitchen equipment.
> And don't forget our special purchase – take home a
> <u>whole case of Beaujolais for just 120 francs!</u>
> Babylone, 40-60, rue René Coty, 75006 Paris (tel. 42-50-50-60)
> Open 10-7, six days a week*
> * closed for national holiday, 14 July

4 COMMENTS ON MODEL ANSWER

1 LAYOUT

The writer has taken plenty of space to lay out the information so that it catches the eye and is easy to read. Babylone's address and the date of the sale are both included. Full marks.

2 CONTENT AND EFFECTIVENESS

The candidate would score high marks here for the following reasons:

- The answer contains all the relevant information from the question, and some additional points.
- It is persuasive, and speaks to tourists, interested in French 'style' - clothes and wine as souvenirs.
- It fulfils its purpose and is quite brief.
- It is clear and readable as all leaflets should be.

QUESTION 1: THE LEAFLET

3 MECHANICAL ACCURACY

No mistakes here: full marks.

This answer is at Distinction level.

5 SECOND ANSWER

> Tourists! You don't usually come in here much, but most of our assistants can manage a few sentences of English. At Babylone we have a summer sale, reductions - 40 per cent off furniture and leather goods, 25-50 per cent off men's and women's summer fashions, 20 per cent off bicycles, sports and camping equipment, chicken equipment, perfumes, There's a special purchase of Beaujolais at 120 francs a case, we want to get rid of that quickly. Our opening hours 10-7 six days a week - See what you can do!

6 COMMENTS ON SECOND ANSWER

1 LAYOUT

- The candidate has grouped the whole answer in one paragraph. This reduces its clarity, and therefore the aim - to inform and to persuade - is not fully achieved.
- Also, the candidate has omitted the address and date. Only people who know Babylone already would know where to find the sale. Even then, they won't know when the sale is happening.

Low marks for layout.

2 CONTENT AND EFFECTIVENESS

- The writer has copied material from the question without thinking about its effect on readers. Tourists will not be impressed to know that 'most of our assistants can manage a few sentences of English', and they may not buy the Beaujolais just because Babylone want 'to get rid of that quickly'. The writer has not thought about what will interest tourists the most, and so the reductions are simply given in the order in which they appear in the question.
- There is nothing in this leaflet to persuade people to come to the sale. The candidate has misunderstood the meaning of 'See what you can do!'. This is a request from the manager to write a leaflet, not a slogan to bring people into Babylone.
- In addition to omitting the address and date, the candidate has failed to mention that Babylone is closed on 14th July.

Low marks again for content and effectiveness.

3 MECHANICAL ACCURACY

- Spelling in this answer is perfect - except for *chicken* instead of *kitchen*.
- The writer has grouped all the information into one paragraph, and has not punctuated correctly. There is a comma, not a full stop at the end of the first sentence, for example.

Not a high score for accuracy.

Once again, a failure.

7 SUMMARY OF COMMON ERRORS

These errors appear regularly in scripts for leaflets. They must be avoided at all costs.

- Not reading the question carefully to know exactly what the examiner requires.
- Omission of name, address and date.
- Not writing the leaflet with the points in it in logical order.
- Not adding sufficient information to that provided in the question.
- Simply copying straight from the question paper.
- Failing to achieve the purpose of the leaflet.
- Failing to use correct English.

QUESTION 1: THE LEAFLET

8 FURTHER PRACTICE

1. Write a **leaflet** intended to be distributed to workers in the book trade, encouraging them to join the National Union of Book Trade Workers.

2. Johannes Prus, the owner of Ludwigshafen Travel Agency, says to you, 'I've just negotiated an excellent deal with all of our hotels for cut-price holidays next summer - the German tour holidays which are patronized mostly by the British. Our tour prices will be ten per cent lower than last summer. Will you draft a **leaflet**, please, that we can send to all our past customers in Britain giving preliminary information about these holidays? Emphasize what terrific bargains they are and tell readers to write in to us for a fully illustrated brochure. This should be really profitable for us.'

3. The General Manager of the mail order toy company for which you work tells you to write a **leaflet** which can be distributed to customers, informing them of the new catalogue which will be issued in a month's time. It will be twice as thick as the current catalogue and contain many bargains.

4. Claude Janvier, General Manager of the company you work for in Lyons, says to you, 'I'm concerned about the increase in stealing there has been in the factory over the last three months. I gather that our factory in the UK has the same problem. I'd like you to draft a **leaflet** that we can issue to all workers telling them of this and that it has got to stop. As from next month - say the tenth - the security guards will have the right to search anyone they suspect may have company goods on them. Anyone caught in possession of stolen goods will be dismissed instantly and reported to the police. Of course, most workers are honest - it's the dishonest few we're after. Before we issue the leaflet here I'll send a copy to our UK subsidiary to get their reaction to it.'

5. Write a **leaflet** that can be given to new employees of the company for which you work, outlining the advantages of having a current account in a bank into which their salaries can be paid every month.

D The notice

1 SAMPLE QUESTION

You are an assistant manager at the Hotel Buon Forchetta, Milan. Your manager, Mauro Cappelletti, says to you one morning, 'We'll have to close the hotel restaurant for two days from tomorrow for repairs to the floor. We can serve a cold buffet lunch to guests in the bar area, but we won't be able to serve dinner. That shouldn't be a problem - there are plenty of restaurants on the Via Pomodoro outside. There are several English and American guests booked in this week. Of course, we'll tell them about the restaurant when they check into the hotel, but I'd like you to write a **notice** for me to put up at the entrance and in the lifts. Otherwise somebody will forget about it and complain. Apologize for the inconvenience to guests. Put it out over my name, will you? Oh, and remind people that we'll serve breakfast in the bar area, as usual.'
Write the required notice.

2 APPROACH

1   You should *read* the notice question, like any other, two or three times so that you know *exactly* what to do. The purpose of the notice is to give information. The information you need for your answer is supplied in the question. Unlike the leaflet, the notice does not try to persuade, and so it is usually briefer. Like the leaflet, it should be quick and simple to read. The notice must also be dated and include the name of the person who wrote it, usually at the bottom. To draw people's attention to it, words like 'Urgent' or 'Important' may be printed at the top in large letters.

   In this question, Mauro Cappelletti is telling his customers that one service his hotel normally offers - the restaurant - will not be provided for two days. It is important that readers are clear about the date, especially as the restaurant will close tomorrow.

2   Decide on the correct *tone* for the notice. Many notices are rather formal and impersonal. Some - particularly warning notices - may have to tell people what they must do. In this case, because the hotel's guests will not be offered the usual service, the notice should apologize and suggest alternatives.

3   Although this will not be a long answer, it is still advisable to *list* the points you will make on the question paper or in your answer book.

4   After writing your answer, *check* as usual for correct grammar, paragraphing, punctuation and spelling.

QUESTION 1: THE NOTICE

3 MODEL ANSWER

> *Hotel Restaurant*
> *Closure, 23-24 April 1992*
>
> We regret that the hotel restaurant will be closed on 23 and 24 April 1992 for repairs to the floor. A cold buffet lunch will be served in the bar area on these days, but dinner will not be served during this period. Guests will find a number of restaurants close to the hotel in the Via Pomodoro.
>
> Breakfast will be served as usual in the bar area.
>
> We apologize to guests for any inconvenience caused.
>
> Mauro Cappelletti
> Manager
> 22 April 1992

4 COMMENTS ON MODEL ANSWER

1 LAYOUT

This answer has a clear heading at the top, the date, and the name and position of the person who wrote it. Full marks.

2 CONTENT AND EFFECTIVENESS

Again, high marks under this heading:
- It contains all the necessary information, without wasting any words.
- The tone is correct - quite formal, and impersonal, but with the necessary apology for inconvenience to guests.
- The purpose is achieved - to catch the eye and to present the message briefly.

3 MECHANICAL ACCURACY

No errors of grammar, paragraphing, punctuation or spelling.

This answer, again, is of Distinction standard.

5 SECOND ANSWER

> For two days from tomorow the hotel restaurant will be close for repairs to the floor. That shouldn't be problem – there are plenty of restaurants on the Via Pomodoro outside. But somebody will forget about it and complain. Apologize for the inconvenience to guests.

6 COMMENTS ON SECOND ANSWER

1 LAYOUT

There is no heading to tell the reader what the notice is about. More importantly, there is no indication of who wrote the notice or when. Guests will not know when *tomorrow* is. Low marks.

2 CONTENT AND EFFECTIVENESS

- Guests will not know when the restaurant will be closed because there is no date. Two other mistakes happened because the candidate did not think before copying material directly from the question:
- It is helpful to point out that there are plenty of restaurants on the Via Pomodoro, but guests will not be pleased to hear that it isn't a problem.
- The comment about someone complaining was clearly not meant to be included in the notice.

3 MECHANICAL ACCURACY

Bad spelling (*tomorrow*...) and grammar (*close* instead of *closed*, omission of *a* before *problem*) will lose marks.

This answer would definitely fail.

QUESTION 1: THE NOTICE

7 SUMMARY OF COMMON ERRORS

The following errors usually lead to failure in this question:

- Not reading the question closely enough to know the examiner's exact requirements.
- Using the wrong tone. An informal tone is not usually appropriate. A warning tone in this case ('Candidates must not try to use the hotel restaurant') would lose marks, as guests simply need to be informed that the restaurant will be closed. But it may be appropriate in other questions, especially where the purpose is to inform readers of any danger.
- Omitting essential information.
- Adding material which is not required by the question.
- Omitting the date and the name of the person issuing the notice.
- As usual, mistakes in grammar, paragraphing, punctuation and spelling.

8 FURTHER PRACTICE

1. You are Administrative Officer of a conference centre, where a major international convention is taking place. Last night, stormy weather damaged a number of major electricity lines in the area. You have been told that there may be power cuts until the necessary repairs are completed. This may take several days.

   Write a **notice** warning guests not to use the lifts at the conference centre. Mention that the reception desk can call porters to help carry anything heavy up and down stairs.

2. You work in the Spanish Souvenirs Store, Seville, which is patronized mainly by British tourists. Write a **notice** to be displayed in the window of the store, informing customers that, as the store will be under new ownership from next Monday, it will be closed for stock-taking and reorganization for three days from that day. When it reopens on Thursday its hours of business will be extended and it will close two hours later every day than it does at present.

3. Sheila Rendell, the Manager of the bank where you work, says to you, 'For the next six Saturday mornings we shall not be opening as the builders will be coming at weekends to build the extension for our Foreign Currency Department. I'm very sorry for the inconvenience it may cause customers but there's nothing I can do to avoid it. If customers *must* visit a bank on Saturday they can temporarily use our High Street Branch, which is about a mile away. It's a nuisance but we shall have to manage as best we can. Would you, please, draw a **notice** we can display letting customers know of these arrangements? Apart from this, business will carry on as usual.'

4. In your capacity as union representative at your company, write a **notice** for the staff noticeboard, requesting your fellow-workers to attend a meeting in the staff recreation room immediately after work one evening this week. You wish to discuss the company's latest pay offer and have a vote on whether or not to accept it. You also wish to have an assistant representative elected to help you as the volume of your union work has increased lately and you are finding it difficult to manage by yourself. Apologize for the necessity of having the meeting at such an inconvenient time for staff.

E The article

1 SAMPLE QUESTION

You run a company group of the Sickness Savings Association and are approached by the Editor of your company's magazine to write an **article** about the benefits to be gained from joining the Association. The article will be read by all the workers as the magazine is distributed to them free.

2 APPROACH

1. *Read* the question carefully so that you know what the *exact* requirements are. The title of the group you run should give you some idea of what it is and does; it collects money from members and in return makes payments to them when they are sick. The article you write will have a readership of people all working for the same company - a restricted readership, as it is called. The object of writing the article is to outline the benefits members gain from the association.

2. On your answer book or the question paper, *list* the benefits that come into your mind without worrying whether or not they are in logical order. When you think you have listed enough benefits put them into logical order (perhaps by numbering them).

3. You want readers to read your article, not ignore it. How do you encourage them to do this? By trying to write an *opening* that will make them want to read on - an arresting opening, as it is called. If you do this they will, hopefully, read the whole article. You then deal with your points one by one and conclude with a statement or question that 'rounds off' the article.

4. As always, **check** your English.

3 MODEL ANSWER

"I'm healthy." "I am never off work." How often do you hear remarks like these? Yet the fact is that sickness can strike anybody – even the most apparently healthy person.

People often tell you that if they are off sick the company still pays their salaries. Yes, they do, but only for nine months; after that no more salary is paid and sick benefit is the only money coming into the house. Even for short illnesses, when the salary is still being paid, all the usual living expenses still occur, and when you are ill you often need little extras, such as special (and often expensive) foods, or a special piece of medical equipment.

What, then, can you do to make certain that if sickness strikes – either on a long-term or a short-term basis – you are free of all financial worries?

The answer is join our company group of the Sickness Savings Association. Many of your fellow-workers are already members and they will all agree that being members relieves them of all financial worries should they unfortunately fall sick.

How does the scheme work? You complete an application form, which can be obtained from me, and pay two per cent of your weekly or monthly salary to the Association. Management are willing to deduct this from salaries to save you the bother of handing over a sum of money to me each pay day. To take an example, if your monthly income is £1,000 you pay only £20 from it.

What benefits do you receive? If you are off sick, you are paid daily the amount you pay monthly. Using the above example, if you pay £20 a month, you receive £20 a day. What a bargain!

In addition to this, financial help is given if you have to pay for dental treatment, if you require spectacles and (for ladies) during pregnancy.

I shall be happy to give you full details of the scheme – without obligation – if you are interested. Just call me on extension 222 at any time during working hours.

Surely, for financial peace of mind during sickness it's worth making a phone call?

QUESTION 1: THE ARTICLE

4 COMMENTS ON MODEL ANSWER

1 LAYOUT

There are no layout requirements as in the other types of question we have dealt with.

2 CONTENT AND EFFECTIVENESS

Bearing in mind that the writer of this article is not a professional journalist, but a company worker contributing to a magazine, this would score highly because:

- It fulfilled its purpose. The reader would be aware of the benefits to be gained from joining the scheme.
- The opening paragraph should attract the attention of most readers.
- The article is structured logically.
- The last brief paragraph rounds off the article by giving the reader something to think about.

3 MECHANICAL ACCURACY

Scores highly here.

A Distinction-level answer, again.

Note

The Editor did not ask for a title, and so none was given. The author did not put a name on the article because the Editor, having asked for the article, would know the author and, when publishing the article, would attribute it to the author.

5 SECOND ANSWER

> I run a company group of the Sickness Savings Association and want to tell you somthing about it. If you are out of work becase you are sick you can get benfit from the association. It does not mater how long you are of sick the benfit will not stop. To join you have to pay a some of money every month and then you get the benfits. It is a very good sceme and a lot of workers are in it. If you see me I will tell you about the sceme and I hope you will join.

6 COMMENTS ON SECOND ANSWER

1 LAYOUT

As mentioned for the model answer, there are no layout requirements as in other types of questions.

2 CONTENT AND EFFECTIVENESS

This piece of work is very poor and will gain few marks for the following reasons:

- It is too short to accomplish what it was supposed to do.
- It is not clear; the writer does not express ideas and thoughts very well.
- There is no 'arresting' beginning to make a reader want to read the rest of the article.
- The writer invites readers to contact him or her about the scheme but does not say how this can be done.
- It does not deal with the subject in logical order.

3 MECHANICAL ACCURACY

There are no paragraphs and there are several spelling errors.

A definite failure.

7 SUMMARY OF COMMON ERRORS

- Not writing exactly what is asked for in the question.
- Not writing an opening that tries to 'hook' the reader.
- Not developing the article in the correct step-by-step, or logical way.
- Either including too much material or not including enough.
- Not finishing by 'rounding off' the article.
- Spelling, punctuation, grammar and paragraphing.

8 FURTHER PRACTICE

1. The General Manager of the company for which you work in Brussels tells you that he has had a request from a British friend for a short **article** on the advantages and (possibly) disadvantages on living in Europe. The article will be read chiefly by British eighteen- to thirty-year-olds.

    Write the appropriate article.

2. Most of the workers at your company have sedentary jobs (jobs that are carried out mostly while sitting down). Write an **article** for the company magazine discussing the importance of sport and exercise for such workers.

3. Write a short **article** for a company/college magazine on the impact of new developments in information technology at your firm or place of education. Suggest what new developments may come in the next ten years.

4. The editor of your company's magazine is running a competition: readers are invited to write articles suggesting ways in which the company could be improved for the benefit of both employees and customers. Write the **article** that you would submit.

5. Write a short **article** for a company/college magazine on the impact of environmental questions at your firm or place of education. Explain what action is being taken, and what action might be needed in the future, to improve environmental awareness.

6. How has the internationalization of world business, for example Japanese overseas investment or the Single European Market, affected your firm or place of education?

    Write a short **article** for a company/college magazine giving details.

QUESTION 2

In this question you are asked to reply to a letter which has been received by the company for which you work. You are also given some extra information. You will need this extra information to write an adequate reply to the letter.

1 SAMPLE QUESTION

Your firm, the UK subsidiary of a major Japanese automobile manufacturer, has received the following letter. Write a correctly laid out letter in reply to it *after* you have read the extract from the minutes of a meeting that follow the letter.

Whitcomb Polytechnic
20-30 Newcastle Road Whitcomb
Tyne & Wear WT5 4AH
tel. 0932-58935
fax 0932-58946

11 October 1991

The General Manager
Fukuoka Motors (UK) Ltd
PO Box 137
York Road
Loughton
Durham
LT3 5HD

Dear Sir

Visit of group of students to Fukuoka Motors

I understand from my colleague, Professor William Jones, who visited your Loughton plant last month, that you sometimes allow groups of students to tour the factory and see for themselves how Japanese production techniques operate in a European environment. Professor Jones himself was most impressed by his own visit, and recommended that I write to you.

Would it be possible for a group of twenty Business Studies students - male and female, aged between 18 and 22 - from Whitcomb Polytechnic to visit you before the end of this term, which is on 21 December? I realise that you must receive many requests for such visits, and that the time available may already be booked up. If it is not, and you are able to see us, I should be most grateful if you could suggest a date and let me know of any normal conditions you lay down for visits of this kind.

I look forward to hearing from you.

Yours faithfully

B Farrant

B Farrant (Dr)
Senior Lecturer

> 7 Plant visits
>   Owing to continued high demand for plant visits from groups of the public, the Committee agreed to fix the following rules for future visits.
>   a) Visits shall take place on Wednesdays only, from 10AM to 5PM.
>   b) Maximum number of people in a group - 15.
>   c) Minimum age of visitors - 16 years.
>   d) Cost of visit: £2.50 per person, including morning coffee, canteen lunch and afternoon tea.
>   e) The guide provided by Fukuoka Motors will be in charge of all groups and must be obeyed at all times.
>   f) The company reserve the right to send off the premises at any time any members of the group who misbehave.
>   Bookings already taken for 1991: 2, 9, 23, 30 October, 13 and 27 November, 5 and 12 December.

2 APPROACH

1 Read the question, in this order:

- the instructions
- the information below the letter
- the letter itself.

Ask yourself 'What does the writer of the letter want?'. When you know (in this case to bring a group of 20 students to visit your company before the end of term) look at the material below the letter again (in this case the extract from the Minutes) to see if what is wanted is possible.

2 Guided by this information, *list the points* you intend to make in your reply (again, either on the question paper or in your answer book). Decide on the *order* in which you wish to make your points.

QUESTION 2

3   Consider the *layout* of your letter. There are six indispensable parts to this:
- your company address
- the date
- the name and address of the person to whom you are writing
- the correct salutation (*Dear Sir* or *Dear Madam* if you don't know who they are: *Dear Dr ..../ Mr ..../ Ms ....* if you do)
- the subscription (*Yours faithfully* after *Dear Sir* or *Dear Madam*:*Yours sincerely* after *Dear Dr ..../ Mr ..../ Ms ....*)
- *either* your own signature with your title (*Mr, Ms, Dr* etc.) in brackets after it and your position in the company *or*, if you have written the letter for someone else to sign, a space for his or her signature and then his or her name printed followed by company position.

Note: the letter that you are given in the question paper will always be laid out correctly. Use this correct layout, as well as the information in the letter, to help you write your own answer.

4   Decide on the *tone* you wish to employ. This should be polite in all cases: rude letters, even when written with very good reason, will annoy the recipient and produce no other desirable result. But there are several different types of polite tone. Here, your aim will be to agree to a request, but to set certain conditions. In other letters, you may need to make a request yourself, or perhaps - in the case of unsatisfactory service or the slow payment of debts - to make a firm demand on the recipient. In each case the type of polite language that you use will be slightly different.

5   Write your letter. As you do so, make sure that you *punctuate* it consistently. For example, at the end of each line of an address except the last, it is quite correct to put *either* a comma *or* nothing. But it is not correct to put a comma at the end of some lines but not others.

6   As usual, when you have completed your answer, *check* carefully your grammar, paragraphing, punctuation and spelling.

3 MODEL ANSWER

Fukuoka Motors (UK) Ltd
PO Box 137 York Road
Loughton Durham LT3 5HD
tel. 0875-272727
fax 0875-277772

15 October 1991

Dr B Farrant
Whitcomb Polytechnic
20-30 Newcastle Road
Whitcomb
Tyne & Wear
WT5 4AH

Dear Dr Farrant

<u>Visit of student group to Fukuoka Motors</u>

Thank you for your letter of 11 October requesting a visit to Fukuoka Motors from a group of twenty Whitcomb Polytechnic students. Unfortunately, our company regulations limit maximum numbers in visiting groups to fifteen. With this in mind, we should be delighted to take a group of your students round the plant on a Wednesday between now and the end of the year. We are already quite booked up, but we would be able to offer you a visit on 6 or 20 November, or 19 December.

We like visiting groups to report to our office at the above address at 10AM. We make a small visiting charge of £2.50 per person: this includes the price of morning coffee, lunch and afternoon tea, all of which are provided by the company. One of our senior staff acts as guide for the group and the visit ends at approximately 5PM.

May I suggest that you telephone my office in the near future to confirm one of the above dates? If none of these is convenient, then perhaps we could arrange a visit for early 1992.

I look forward to hearing from you.

Yours sincerely

(sign your own name here)

(write your own name here)
<u>General Manager</u>

QUESTION 2

4 COMMENTS ON MODEL ANSWER

1 LAYOUT

Full marks as everything is laid out correctly. The candidate has chosen to leave out commas in the addresses, and has stuck to this throughout: punctuation is therefore consistent.

2 CONTENT AND EFFECTIVENESS

The letter would score highly under this heading for the following reasons:

- All the necessary information is given. The candidate has studied and used the information on plant visits to give details on dates, times, and other arrangements.

- The information is given in a logical order. The three major points are given first: the problem about group numbers, the possibility of a visit, and the dates available. The detailed arrangements follow in the second part of the letter.

- The writer is clear on the further action to be taken, and asks Dr Farrant to confirm a date.

- The tone is polite and courteous. The writer has indicated that a company guide will take charge of the students, but has not felt it necessary to say that the guide 'must be obeyed'.

3 MECHANICAL ACCURACY

No errors: high marks.

This answer merits a Distinction.

5 SECOND ANSWER

The General Manager
Fukuoka Motors (UK)
PO Box 137
York Road
Loughton
Durham

11th of October 1991

Dr B Farrant
Whitcomb Polytechnic,
20-30 Newcastle Road,
Whitcomb
Tyne & Wear
WTS 4AH

Dear Mr. Farrant

Thanks for your letter of 11th of October. We welcome the visit of your group of students any time between now and the end of your term except 2, 9, 23, 30 October, 13, 27 November, 5, 12 December.

The guide provided by Fukuoka Motors will be in charge of all groups and must be obeyed at all times. The company reserve the right to send off the premises at any time any members of the group who misbehave.

Cost of visit: £2.50 per person, including morning coffee, canten lunch and afternoon tea.

I hope to meet you soon.

Yours faithfully

Mr Toshihiro Hirano

6 COMMENTS ON SECOND ANSWER

1 LAYOUT

Mistakes here include:
- The sender's title is above the address, not below his name.
- B Farrant is called *Mr* not *Dr* at the beginning of the letter.
- There is no consistency in the use of commas in the layout.
- There is no consistent style for dates.
- The writer put *Mr* before his own name, not after it in brackets.
- The writer put *Yours faithfully*, instead of *Yours sincerely* after *Dear Mr Farrant*.

2 CONTENT AND EFFECTIVENESS

Low marks here because:
- Vital information is omitted. The writer fails to mention that only 15 students are allowed in a group, and that visits are only possible on Wednesdays. Details on visiting times are also left out.
- The tone is not appropriate. In the first paragraph it is too relaxed and informal (*Thanks*, instead of *Thank you*). In the second paragraph the writer has copied from the information given: the effect is the opposite of welcoming.
- The writer is not clear about the next step to take: he merely looks forward to meeting Dr Farrant at an unspecified date.

3 MECHANICAL ACCURACY

The writer has been fairly careful in copying material from the information given. However, he has not realised that full sentences are required in this type of letter: there is no verb in the last paragraph. And *Canteen* is spelt incorrectly.
Despite *relatively* good mechanical accuracy, this letter would still fail.

7 SUMMARY OF COMMON ERRORS

- Incorrect layout. This can easily be avoided by using the correctly laid out letter on the question paper as a model.
- The date on the letter being the same as the date on the question paper.
- Not reading, understanding, and using, the instructions and information given to you when writing your letter of reply.
- Giving insufficient information in the letter.
- Mistakes of grammar, paragraphing, punctuation and spelling.

8 FURTHER PRACTICE

1 Write a suitable reply to the following letter which has been received by your company, Marco Gardini's, after you have read the advertisement following the letter.

> 12 Mill Street
> Taunton
> Somerset
> SS12 3BQ
> England
>
> 10 September 1990
>
> Mr Ettore Galli
> Marco Gardini (UK) Ltd
> 73 Brook Street
> London
> W2B 3CD
>
> Dear Mr Galli
>
> Application for the post of Regional Sales Manager
>
> I am writing to apply for the post of Regional Sales Manager (South-West England) with Marco Gardini UK advertised in the Daily Telegraph on 6 September 1990. As requested, I am enclosing a brief résumé.
>
> I believe that my experience and contacts in the furniture industry would contribute considerably to the future success of Marco Gardini in this country. I also feel that my success in previous and current posts have prepared me for a career move involving greater responsibility.
>
> I would be happy to supply the names of referees on request. In the meantime, I very much hope that you will be able to consider my application.
>
> Yours sincerely
>
> *Maria Glover*
>
> Maria Glover (Ms)

QUESTION 2

```
Name:            Maria Francesca Glover

Address:         12 Mill Street, Taunton,
                 Somerset SS12 3BQ, England
                 (tel. 0823-87598)

Date of birth: 18 August 1962

Qualifications

GCE A-levels: French, Italian, Art

Degree in Modern Languages, Bristol Polytechnic

Fluent Italian maintained during visits to
family in Italy

Experience

1984-1988:       Junior Salesperson, IK Furniture
                 Ltd., Bristol

1988-present:    Deputy Assistant Manager
                 (furniture), Habitat-Mothercare
                 Ltd., Oxford
```

Regional Sales Manager
(South-West England)

Around 18K with commission and generous benefits package

We are a fast-expanding Italian furniture supplier with a growing number of wholesale and retail customers in the UK. Following the reorganization of our UK sales force, we are looking for a young, dynamic person with relevant experience in the industry to develop new markets in the South-West, and to manage a team of two reps. Good Italian would be an advantage, as the successful candidate will pay regular visits to our head office in Milan.

Phone Ettore Galli on 01-375-4661 for further details, or write with a brief résumé to **Ettore Galli, Marco Gardini (UK) Ltd., 73 Brook Street, London W2B 3CD.**

QUESTION 2

2 Your company has received the following letter from a customer in the UK. Write a correctly laid out letter in reply to it *after you have read the notes below the letter.*

Easigro Garden Centres Ltd
Oakley Road, Caverton, Berks RG3 5BU
Tel. 0643-75672

23 May 1991

Mr Peter Jacobmeyer
Sales Manager
Bleckenbauer GmbH
Schillerstrasse 87
6800 Mannheim 23
West Germany

Dear Mr Jacobmeyer

<u>Confirmation of chain saw order</u>

I am writing to confirm my order placed by telephone today for the following items:

25 BB 1315 chain saws

40 BB 1727 chain saws.

Our customers have been very pleased with both of these models, which have sold extremely well at all five of our outlets in the southern UK. I therefore anticipate further substantial orders in the near future. For this reason, I would be very glad of the opportunity to discuss revised credit terms and discounts with a view to expanding our volume of business.

Are you, or a colleague, likely to visit Britain in the near future? I would be grateful to hear your views on this matter.

Yours sincerely

Cliff Roberts

Cliff Roberts
<u>General Manager</u>

Peter Jacobmeyer's reaction to the letter was cautious. 'Listen', he said to you, 'we need to be careful on this one. Roberts still hasn't paid us for his January order, so he's well over the usual 90 days' credit. It was quite a big order, too - over DM20,000. We simply can't send him more goods until he settles on what he's already had - it's company policy, and I can't change that. But he's our best customer in Britain, and he's promising more expansion, so we can't just write and tell him to pay up if he wants more goods. Look - draft a letter and tell him I'll be in England on 12 and 13 June, and I'll try to see him then. And in the meantime, sorry, we can't meet his order till he settles his account. The letter should go out over my name. Thanks'.

QUESTION 3

The syllabus of the English for Business Second Level Examination says that Question 3 consists of 'A *reformulation* task requiring candidates to expand, reduce or selectively rewrite a passage of English for some defined purpose within a given role'.

The following section of the book is divided into:

A   Reduction

B   Expansion

A   Reduction

1 SAMPLE QUESTION

The Sales Manager of Stanton's Business Agency, for which you work, says to you, 'We want to produce a short **leaflet** for prospective shop purchasers, giving them some advice on shop-opening hours. I'd like you to write a leaflet, please. Use some of the important points made in this leaflet, which is too long for our purpose, to write your one.' Complete the task.

> When you are your own boss you can please yourself about the time of starting work. But do not expect to make a fortune if the hours are erratic, with the Closed sign on the door at times customers may reasonably expect your shop to be open. Shopkeepers with that kind of attitude will soon be out of business, and they will probably wonder why they were so unsuccessful when a couple who are prepared to work take over the business. Shopkeepers must give good service if they want to succeed - and who doesn't? But there are apparently people who take over a shop and do not understand their responsibilities to the public. If you adopt a don't-care manner to the customers they will soon find another shop.
>
>   Do not expect the till to be overflowing with money early in the morning, but the fact that you are open and giving service is important. Unless the shop is in a very favoured position the takings will not be particularly exciting before 8.30 or 9 a.m.
>
>   Some shops make a routine of closing promptly at 6 p.m. I don't. While trade is there my shops are open until 8 p.m., seven days a week. It gives the commuters time to make their purchases and usually they become regular customers, which means that you will attract the profitable weekend sales. Those two hours in the evening can have a vital influence on receipts for a shop on an estate or in a secondary position. But it is necessary to do a little experimenting on the potential before deciding on the closing hours. If the area is consistently quiet after 6 p.m. there is no point in keeping open for one or two casual customers.
>
>   High Street shops are different because most people have finished shopping by 5.30 or 6 p.m. So I follow the trend and close when there is no business around. People are not milling around High Street shops after 6 p.m. because there is no point in staring at a shuttered door. Shops in this type of district also close on Sundays but newsagents are an exception, especially if papers are delivered. The boys have to be sent on their rounds and the shop should stay open until the papers have been sold, usually about noon.

2 APPROACH

1. *Read the question* a few times until you understand precisely what the examiner requires. In our example you are asked to read a leaflet and to compose a shorter one from it which will be useful for people considering buying a shop. You will have noticed that this is really an exercise in summary writing.

2. Read the passage once to get a *general idea* of what it is about. Our example deals with the opening hours of shops.

3. Now read the passage *several times*. Underline or highlight the main points. You may find it useful to delete illustrative examples, as you will not need them.

4. Note the *order* in which you wish to make the points. This may be the same order as in the passage: or you may decide to change it. You should add a title to your work, and give some indication of who has issued it. But do not include any points or ideas that are not in the original passage.

5. Write your first draft.

6. Compare what you have written with the original passage to make sure that you have not omitted anything essential.

7. If you are satisfied with your first draft, then write your final version. In our example, a leaflet to be read by prospective shop buyers is required, so it must be easily readable and in a courteous tone.

8. Check grammar, paragraphing, punctuation and spelling.

QUESTION 3: REDUCTION

3 MODEL ANSWER

> <u>Shop opening hours</u>
>
> To make a success of your shop you must be open at reasonable times and have a sense of responsibility towards your customers.
>
> Although business may not be brisk early in the morning, unless you are in a good trading spot, you should be open for those few customers who may wish to patronize you.
>
> Before deciding when to close, carry out some investigations in the area the shop serves to see if it is worth your while financially to stay open later than 6 p.m., the normal closing time. In some areas commuters like to shop up to, say, 8 p.m. and often become regular customers of the shop that stays open.
>
> If your shop is in a main shopping area, it is normal to close by 6 p.m. because few shoppers are around after that time. Sunday closing is the rule unless you have a newsagent's shop selling Sunday newspapers.
>
> <u>Issued by Stanton's Business Agency, 5 High Street, Leeds GH4 6MM</u>

4 COMMENTS ON MODEL ANSWER

1 LAYOUT

High marks here as it has a title and looks pleasing to the eye. It also shows who issued the leaflet.

2 CONTENT AND EFFECTIVENESS

This section would also gain high marks:

- It contains all the main points of the longer leaflet.
- It is not simply copied from the longer leaflet - one of the commonest errors in this type of question.
- Contains nothing, apart from the title and name and address, that was not in the original.

3 MECHANICAL ACCURACY

No spelling errors. No language mistakes. High score.
A Distinction.

5 SECOND ANSWER

When you are your own boss you can please yourself about the times of starting work. But do not expect to make a fortune. Shopkeepers with that attitude will soon be out of business. But there are apparently people who take over a shop and do not understand their responsibilities.

Do not expect the till to be overflowing with money early in the morning.

Some shops make a routine of closing promptly at 6 p.m. I don't. While trade is there my shops are open until 8 p.m. seven days a week.

High Street shops are different because most people have finished shopping by 5.30 or 6 p.m.. So I follow the trend and close when there is no business around. Shops in this type of district also close on Sundays.

6 COMMENTS ON SECOND ANSWER

1 LAYOUT

Few marks here: the leaflet has no title, and no indication of who has produced it.

2 CONTENT AND EFFECTIVENESS

Very few marks here, because:

- The answer is copied from the original with no attempt at putting the material into different words. This is one of the commonest causes of failure in this type of question.
- The copying did not make sense, and so the finished leaflet did not achieve its purpose of helping prospective purchasers of shops.
- The candidate clearly did not understand the purpose of the task. Better understanding might have been achieved if more time had been spent on reading the question carefully.

3 MECHANICAL ACCURACY

This piece of work, unlike many previous Second Answers, is not full of spelling errors. The candidate has copied carefully from the question paper. However, scoring quite well under this heading does not compensate for low marks gained under previous headings.

This answer is still, therefore, a failure.

B Expansion

1 SAMPLE QUESTION

Your General Manager, Dan Levin, says to you, 'This has just arrived from Arnold Schlegel. He's one of our biggest customers, and I don't want to miss him, but I can't cancel my trip to Spain, and I won't be back till 16 July. Get Paul Fontana to handle it, will you? Leave a memo on his desk, under my name. Tell him to drop everything, contact Schlegel, ask him over here, show him round the factory. Perhaps he can stay around till I get back - that would be great. Tell Paul to try and fix it. If he can't, Paul should just listen to what he's got to say, but not make any commitment. Apologize to Paul for me. And I'll get back to Schlegel as soon as I can'.

```
ARRIVING HEATHROW 10 JULY. STAYING HILTON 4 DAYS.
AUSTRIAN MARKET FOR YOUR PRODUCTS BOOMING. BIG NEW
ORDERS POSSIBLE BUT MUST DISCUSS PRICES DISCOUNTS
PAYMENT TERMS AND PACKAGING. PLEASE CONTACT SOONEST.

SCHLEGEL
```

Complete the task.

2 APPROACH

In the last exercise you had to reduce the passage given. Here you have to expand the information you are given. In this example you have to write a memo.

1 *Read the question* until you are absolutely clear in your mind what you have to do. In this example you have to make sure that Paul Fontana gives an important customer the attention that he is clearly expecting. Fontana should not, however, negotiate any special deals with Schlegel. Anything of that kind must wait till Levin returns.

2 Recall the correct *form* of the document you are producing - here a memo.

3 Note the points you wish to make and put them in order. You may add some extra information if you wish.

4 Check grammar, paragraphing, punctuation and spelling.

QUESTION 3: EXPANSION   53

3 MODEL ANSWER

> From: Dan Levin   Date: 9 July 1991
>
> To: Paul Fontana   Subject: Arnold Schlegel's visit, 10-13 July
>
> A telex from Arnold Schlegel has just arrived, saying he's in London from tomorrow to 13 July and wants to see us. I'm off to Spain so I'd like you to drop everything and deal with it. I'm sorry to do this to you, but Schlegel's a very important customer. He thinks he can get big new orders in Austria but he wants to talk about prices and discounts, and payment terms, and packaging. Could you contact him at the Hilton and arrange for him to come and talk? Show him round the factory and listen to his proposals, but don't commit us to anything. And try and get him to stay till 16 July. I'll be back then and we could meet. Otherwise let him know I'll get back to him as soon as I'm in the office. And give him my regards.
>
> Many thanks for doing this.
>
> DL

4 COMMENTS ON MODEL ANSWER

1 LAYOUT

Full marks for correct layout of memo.

2 CONTENT AND EFFECTIVENESS

This would receive high marks for the following reasons:
- It briefs Paul Fontana clearly on the problem of Schlegel's unexpected arrival, and why he should be given the attention he wants.
- It contains all the information required for Fontana to look after Schlegel.
- It reads smoothly.

3 MECHANICAL ACCURACY

No mistakes, high marks.
Distinction level.

5 SECOND ANSWER

> From: Dan Levin
>
> To: Paul Fontana
>
> Schlegel is arriving tomorow at Heathrow. He's a good costomer, so contact him to talk about prices, discounts, payment terms and packaging. Show him round the factory. Apologize to Paul for me. And I'll get back to Schlegel as soon as I can'.

6 COMMENTS ON SECOND ANSWER

1 LAYOUT

The writer has omitted both date and subject.

2 CONTENT AND EFFECTIVENESS

This would receive few marks because:

- It gives insufficient information on why Schlegel's visit is important.
- It gives no indication of why Fontana, not Levin, should deal with it.
- It gives Levin no guidance as to where to contact Schlegel.
- It fails to tell Fontana not to negotiate with Schlegel.

3 MECHANICAL ACCURACY

Tomorrow and *Customer* misspelt. An unnecessary inverted comma at the end of the memo.

Once again, a fail.

7 SUMMARY OF COMMON ERRORS

- Failing to understand exactly what is required by the examiner.
- In reducing a passage, including material not in the original passage, as well as irrelevant material such as illustrative examples.
- Copying extensively from the question without understanding what is being copied.
- Failing to consider the order in which points should be made.
- Mistakes of grammar, paragraphing, punctuation and spelling.

QUESTION 3: EXPANSION

8 FURTHER PRACTICE

1 Your firm, President Electronics, is recruiting a London-based Area Manager in order to expand sales of your personal computers (PCs) in the UK market. Your boss, Peter Phang, says to you, 'I'd like you to write a description of the job for people who enquire about it. You know the sort of person we want. We'll need somebody with first-class technical knowledge and plenty of experience of the computer industry, especially PCs. The ideal thing would be someone who knows our own products already. But I know that may not be possible - we're not very well known in Britain. If they don't know our PCs, though, they should be ready to find out about them fast: we need someone who can spend a week in our plants in Asia and go back to the UK knowing our complete product range inside-out.

'We don't want anyone too old. We need someone with plenty of energy and new ideas. Someone mobile, too. The person we get is going to have to do a lot of travelling - all round the UK, for a start. And there'll be several trips a year to Hong Kong and Singapore.

'What else? It has to be someone with experience on the sales side. They'll need to know plenty about wholesaling and retailing PCs in the UK. And with a proven record of success in some area of selling - that means fixing an ambitious budget and meeting it. Someone who knows what the competition's doing - and someone who can keep up with new market trends and give us advice on new product development.

'Oh yes, and we do want somebody who knows about being a *manager*. We'll want the new person to start recruiting sales reps pretty quickly. So they'll need to be able to motivate subordinates to work as a team. If we really get off the ground in the UK, then we could be selling into the whole of Europe in about 3 years. Then we'll really need a network of salespeople.

'I think that's about it. Oh - mention the salary, of course: about £23,000 with a car, and commission, and benefits. Applications with full CV to me at PO Box 4763, London SW1A 3AD, by 5 November 1991. And we'll talk to shortlisted candidates at the Dorchester Hotel in London on 26 November. OK?'

Write the job description to be sent out to candidates.

2 You arrive at your office one morning and find the following Telephone Message form on your desk. Deal with it, inventing information where necessary.

For	Office Manager	From	John Stephens, UK Head Office
Telephone	#6-101		

Mr Stephens would like a quick report on Joanna White, the UK management trainee they sent us last month. Apparently there have been problems with some of the trainees in other branches, and Mr Stephens asked if everything was OK here. He doesn't want a detailed report, but he wants to know about Joanna White's punctuality, attendance, reliability, and relationships with staff. Also - is she learning anything, is she at all useful, and would you employ her on a permanent basis?

Mr Stephens will be in meetings most of today, so it won't be easy to phone him. Could you fax him a quick memo - as soon as you can?

Date	6 Dec. 1990	**Time**	0915
Call received by	Anna Morandi		

London Chamber of Commerce and Industry Examinations

How to make contact

Address The London Chamber of Commerce and Industry
Examinations Board
Marlowe House
Station Road
Sidcup
Kent
DA15 7BJ
England

Telephone (from within UK)   081 302 0261
(from outside UK) +44 81 302 0261

Telex 888941 LCCIG ATTN EXAMS BOARD

Facsimile (from within UK)   081 302 4169
(from outside UK) +44 81 302 4169

If you need	Contact ....
1 Information or advice on the English for Business or English for Commerce examinations of the LCCI, or on examining centres	Dr G D Pickett Examinations Officer Languages and EFL
2 Past papers of the examinations	Publications Department
3 Details of the Spoken English for Industry and Commerce (SEFIC) oral examination	Dr G D Pickett
4 General information on the LCCI Commercial Education Scheme and Examination Board, or on examinations other than English for Business or English for Commerce	Publications Department
5 More detailed information on specific, non-English examinations	The relevant Examinations Officer